# Communications

Brian Williams

# www.heinemann.co.uk/library

Visit our website to find out more information about Heinemann Library books.

To order:

 Phone 44 (0) 1865 888066

 Send a fax to 44 (0) 1865 314091

 Visit the Heinemann Bookshop at www.heinemann.co.uk/library to browse our catalogue and order online.

First published in Great Britain by Heinemann Library, Halley Court, Jordan Hill, Oxford OX2 8EJ, a division of Reed Educational and Professional Publishing Ltd. Heinemann is a registered trademark of Reed Educational & Professional Publishing Limited.

OXFORD MELBOURNE AUCKLAND JOHANNESBURG BLANTYRE
GABORONE IBADAN PORTSMOUTH NH (USA) CHICAGO

© Reed Educational and Professional Publishing Ltd 2001
The moral right of the proprietor has been asserted.

Designed by Tinstar Design (www.tinstar.co.uk)
Originated by Ambassador Litho Ltd
Printed in Hong Kong/China

ISBN 0 431 13240 2
05 04 03 02 01
10 9 8 7 6 5 4 3 2 1

British Library Cataloguing in Publication Data
Williams, Brian, 1943
    Communications. – (Great Inventions)
    1. Mass Media
    I. Title
    384

Acknowledgements
The Publishers would like to thank the following for permission to reproduce photographs:
AKG London: pp7, 12, 30, Erich Lessing pp6, 14, British Library pp8, 13; Corbis: pp4, 5, 17, 22, 26, 32, 34, 37; Culture Archive: p16; Ericsson: p41; Mary Evans Picture Library: pp10, 27, 28; Photodisc: p35; Potrset systems Ltd p23; Popperfoto: Reuters p43; Science and Society: Science Museum pp24, 25, 30, 31, 33, 38; Science Photo Library: pp18 (x2), 29, NASA p9, Rosenfeld Images Ltd p11, Ben Johnson p21, Robert Isear p23, Julian Baum p39

Cover photographs: Photodisc (l and t), Ancient Art & Architecture (r)

Every effort has been made to contact copyright holders of any material reproduced in this book. Any omissions will be rectified in subsequent printings if notice is given to the Publisher.

Any words appearing in the text in bold, **like this**, are explained in the Glossary.

# Contents

# Introduction

Communication means the exchange and storage of information. If you say to someone 'my name is Sarah', you are passing on information. The person you speak to needs to know the **code** – how to understand the sounds you say – your language. He or she can remember, or store, the information in their memory. You can pass on information in other ways – by writing your name, by sending an email, or by waving flags!

## How we communicate

Animals communicate in all kinds of ways. Birds sing to tell other birds that 'this is my tree, keep away'. A dog bares its teeth to show fear or aggression. Animals as different as a bee and a chimpanzee communicate using sounds and movements of their bodies.

*The Rosetta Stone, bearing fragments of 2000-year-old text in three forms of writing, solved the riddle of Egyptian hieroglyphics. Found half-buried in 1799, it is now in the British Museum, London.*

However, only humans have complex languages, which can be expressed in speech and written down as words and numbers. We often use wordless communication too – when we smile, nod, wave or shake hands. Watch when two people meet and begin talking – notice how their hands move, how their body posture alters. This body language is part of the way people communicate.

## Passing on knowledge

Special communication skills make people different from animals. From prehistoric times, humans passed on what they had learned. At first, this was done by speech, through stories, repeated and added to over many generations. Over the last 5000 years people have invented new forms of communication. The most important was writing.

## Communications inventions

Inventors tried many ingenious ways to make communications easier, more accurate and faster. Even the pencil had to be invented! Communications inventions such as the book and the printing press spread knowledge. Others, like the typewriter and fax machine, became business aids.

In the past 150 years, there has been a revolution in communications, which have become so fast that they make the world seem much smaller. In 1800, it took two weeks for a letter to travel from Europe to the USA by ship. Today, we can pick up the phone to call a friend any time of day, or send an email. Computers store incredible amounts of information, which can be sent around the world in a split second. We can watch live television pictures by **satellite** from anywhere in the world.

In the 21st century communications are changing faster than at any time in history. It's hard to predict what will happen next!

*In the 21st century, mobile phones and small carry-anywhere laptop computers have made instant communication possible. We can talk and send messages to practically any place in the world.*

# Writing, 3500BC

Writing is 'organized' speech, a system of marks that represent the sounds people make when they speak. Prehistoric people began to speak many thousands of years ago. Writing was invented much later, about 5500 years ago. With writing, civilization and recorded history began.

## Picture-making

Before people learned to write, they drew pictures – with a stick in the sand, or by daubing coloured mud on a rock. More than 15,000 years ago, prehistoric people living in caves drew pictures of the animals they hunted for food.

*The Sumerians wrote on tablets of soft clay using a wedge-shaped tool. The writers, called scribes, had to memorise more than 500 different signs.*

## The first writing

A great change happened about 10,000 years ago. Groups of people in South-west Asia, Egypt and China gave up hunting and became farmers. They settled in villages, which grew into towns. Farmers traded food and things they made, such as clay pots, with their neighbours. They needed a system of record-keeping. How many goats did A have last year? How many goats did A give B in exchange for B's sacks of grain?

The inventors of writing (several people in more than one place) realized that pictures alone could not communicate enough information. The Sumerians, who lived in what is now Iraq, used numbers for counting, and in about 3500BC they invented other **signs** that stood for sounds, groups of sounds, or words. For example, a picture of a cat meant 'cat'. But a cat-picture could also stand for the sound 'cat', so it could be used in other words, such as 'catch'. Picture-signs became sound-signs – what we now call letters.

## Sumerian writing

The Sumerians wrote on small tablets of soft clay, using a pointed reed or stick to make marks, some round and others wedge-shaped. The shapes give this writing its name: *cuneiform* (wedge-shaped).

What did these first writers write about? Mostly it was business. They listed the numbers of animals on their farms and the sacks of wheat in their granaries. When the moist clay dried in the sun, it hardened, and so the lists could be kept safe for years. Some of these ancient clay writings still exist, 5000 years later.

## Alphabets

About 3000BC, the Egyptians developed a form of writing called **hieroglyphics**. They wrote 24 signs standing for letters or single-letter words. It was a kind of alphabet.

By about 4000 years ago there were several alphabets. The one we use, with 26 letters standing for different sounds, came from the Greeks, who probably copied theirs from the **Phoenicians**. The name alphabet comes from the Greek words for A (alpha) and B (beta). Writing was used to record all kinds of information – laws, taxes, trade, religion, science, history, family letters, plays and poetry.

*People write their names as personal signs, or signatures. This is the signature of the German composer Johann Sebastian Bach (1685–1750), with his 'job title'.*

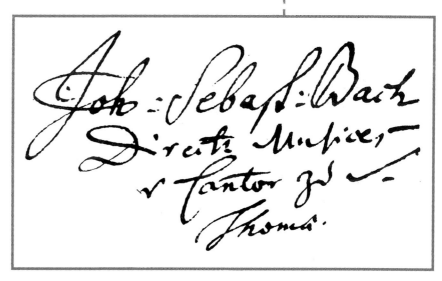

| 3500–3000BC | 3000BC | BEFORE 1400BC | 2000BC | 1000BC | 600BC |
|---|---|---|---|---|---|
| CUNEIFORM WRITING IN SUMERIA | HIEROGLYPHIC WRITING IN EGYPT | CHINESE CHARACTERS | PHOENICIAN ALPHABET DEVELOPED | GREEK ALPHABET USED | LATIN ALPHABET USED |

# Maps, 2300BC

Prehistoric hunters made long journeys, perhaps marking the way for others by cuts in the bark of trees. They had no maps, other than in their memory, stored with familiar landmarks such as fallen trees. They found their way by the sun and stars.

## Why make maps?

We do not know who made the first map. The oldest we have was drawn on a clay tablet 3000 years ago in Babylon, then a great empire (its ruins are now within Iraq). This ancient map shows villages, rivers and mountains. The villages are the key to why the map was made. People had become farmers, living in villages, and were trading with people in neighbouring villages. A map could show the safe route from one village to the next. It could also record information, such as showing which farmers owned which fields. The local ruler used field-maps to record who should pay taxes on land.

## Babylonians and Egyptian map-makers

*A world map of 1482, based on the maps of the Greek geographer Ptolemy, who lived about AD 150.*

The Babylonians, who were excellent mathematicians, drew the first maps. They were the first people to divide a circle into 360 degrees – just as on a modern map the Earth is divided into lines of **latitude** and **longitude**.

The Egyptians also made good maps, using **geometry** to survey the land. Every year the Nile River flooded its banks and washed away farmers' boundary markers. Checking the maps settled arguments.

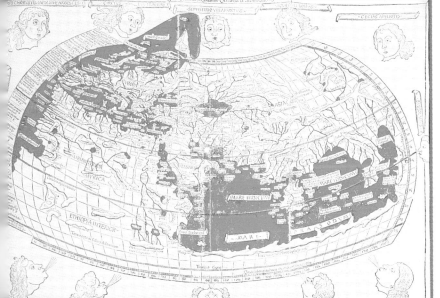

## World maps

By 400BC the Ancient Greeks were sailing across the Mediterranean Sea on trading voyages. Sailors and settlers made maps of this wider world – the Mediterranean islands, the coasts of North Africa and southern Europe, and the lands of the Middle East.

Greek geographers worked out that the Earth must be round and used geometry to calculate very accurately how big it was. Many ordinary people still believed the Earth was flat, and feared sailors could fall off the edge!

Europeans still had nothing better than Greek world maps 2000 years later. When Christopher Columbus set sail in 1492, he expected to reach Asia in a day or so. Finding the USA in the way was a big surprise!

Each new voyage of exploration brought more information to improve maps. Using this knowledge in a new way, European map-maker Gerardus Mercator drew the first really accurate world map in 1569. Surveyors explored the world, mapping mountains, rivers and deserts. The science of map-making became more accurate in the 1920s with air photography and in the 1960s with **satellites** in space.

*Satellites began to map the Earth in the 1960s. Photos taken from spacecraft gave people their first ever view of the entire planet.*

**Gerardus Mercator (1512–94)**
Mercator was the greatest map-maker of the 1500s. He was born in Flanders (now Belgium). He made globes and flat maps drawn to scale on sheets marked by grid lines. Mercator was the first to draw the round Earth accurately on a flat map. The several different ways of doing this are called projections. Distances between places on a Mercator map were roughly correct, although the shapes of continents were distorted. Mercator also produced the first atlas, or collection of maps.

| 3000BC | 2300BC | 1570 | 1686 | 1855 | 1960s |
|---|---|---|---|---|---|
| EGYPTIANS INVENT LAND SURVEYING | OLDEST KNOWN MAP, FROM SUMERIA | FIRST BOOK OF MAPS, OR ATLAS | FIRST WEATHER MAP, DRAWN BY ENGLISH ASTRONOMER SIR EDMOND HALLEY | FIRST STATISTICAL MAPS – SHOWING CHOLERA DEATHS IN LONDON | SPACE SATELLITES TRANSFORM MAP-MAKING |

# Paper, AD 105

The Roman emperor Julius Caesar never wrote on paper. Many Ancient Romans used wax tablets for sending letters to one another. After reading a wax-tablet letter, a Roman smoothed the wax and wrote an answer. It was a great way to recycle!

## Papyrus

Writing on clay or wax tablets was inconvenient, though. The tablet was heavy to carry and broke if you dropped it. (People used broken pots to scrawl notes or shopping lists on.) There was another writing material, called papyrus, made from reeds. Reed stems were soaked in water and squashed in layers to make a white papery material, which was cut into sheets or rolled onto wooden rods. Papyrus reeds were also used to make mats and sandals. Only those people trained to read and write (called scribes) used papyrus for writing.

## Parchment

Papyrus reeds grew along the River Nile in Egypt and only the Egyptians made papyrus. Everyone else had to buy it from them. About 200BC, the Egyptians stopped selling papyrus to the King of Pergamum in Asia Minor. The king ordered his cleverest inventors to come up with an alternative. They produced a new writing material made from the skins of sheep, calves and goats. Called parchment, it lasted longer than papyrus and was cheaper.

*Chinese papermakers at work. They mixed plant fibres with water and then dried the pulp on screens.*

## How paper was invented

Paper was invented by the Chinese in about AD 105. The huge Chinese Empire was run by thousands of officials, who carried out the emperor's commands by exchanging thousands of letters, written on parchment or silk. This cost too much, and the emperor told his experts to find a cheaper writing material.

An official named Tsai Lun came up with the answer. Maybe he had watched wasps building a paper nest. He mashed together mulberry tree bark, bamboo fibres, hemp, flax and water until he had a soggy paste or pulp. He spread the pulp thinly over a mesh of woven bamboo, and let it dry. The result was a sheet of paper. Even old fishing nets or rags could be made into paper. The cheapest paper was too coarse to write on. Chinese painters preferred smooth silk. But cheap paper was useful for wrapping and clothing.

*In a modern paper mill, wood pulp is the most common raw material. The dried paper flows out and is rolled onto huge reels.*

## The secret leaks out

For the next 500 years the Chinese were the only people making paper. News of their invention spread only after Chinese paper-makers were captured by foreigners. Paper-making reached the Middle East by AD 800, and by the end of the 12th century, Crusaders returning from fighting in the Holy Land (Palestine) had brought the secret to Europe. Soon paper mills with water-driven machinery were hard at work pulping rags for paper. In the 1450s came an invention that needed lots of paper – the printed book.

| 3000BC | 150BC | AD 105 | 1100s | 1860s | 1940s |
|---|---|---|---|---|---|
| PAPYRUS USED IN EGYPT | LONGER-LASTING PARCHMENT STARTS TO REPLACE PAPYRUS | FIRST PAPER MADE IN CHINA | PAPER-MAKING REACHES EUROPE | FIRST PAPER BAGS | RECYCLING OR REUSE OF WASTE PAPER BEGINS. RECYCLING BECOMES WIDESPREAD FROM THE 1970s |

# Book, 350

The first books were not at all like modern paperbacks. For a start, they were not printed. In Ancient Rome, for example, all books were written by hand, usually on long strips of parchment or papyrus rolled onto wooden rods. To read this kind of book, you unwound the roll, or **scroll**.

*The library at Alexandria, Egypt, in the 3rd century BC, shown here in a 19th-century engraving, had over 400,000 scroll-books.*

In the AD 300s the Romans invented a new kind of book, with pages, called a codex. This was the first book that looked like a modern book. Handwritten parchment sheets were sewn and glued together between wood and leather covers. Some books were too big to be rolled on a single scroll – the Bible, for instance. One codex could contain the whole of the Bible, though the result was a very big and heavy book, which took many hours of skilled work to make.

## Books in the Middle Ages

In the Middle Ages (from AD 500 to 1500), books were so precious that they were often kept chained to desks to stop people stealing them. Each copy was made by hand, usually by monks in monasteries. The pages were decorated with beautiful hand-painted pictures and ornate letters.

A form of printing, using inked wooden blocks, was invented in China and Korea before AD 800. It was slow, producing one page at a time. The earliest known printed book is a Chinese book of **Buddhist** teachings called the *Diamond Sutra*, made in AD 868.

Most early books were either religious (like the Bible) or historical. In Europe before 1500, most books were written in Latin. One of the first books written in English was a history of England, called the *Anglo-Saxon Chronicle*, begun in the 9th century.

## Who read books?

Before about 1500, few people ever learned to read and write, so not many people owned books. The printing press (1454) made books cheaper but even printed books were bound by hand – sometimes this was done after you bought the book! After 1500, more people went to school or learned to read at home. These new readers wanted handy-sized books, about everyday subjects (such as poetry, cookery and medicine) as well as big Bibles and other religious books. Publishing companies began to pay authors and sell books. After 1820, steam printing machines began turning out cheap books in cloth and card covers by the millions.

## Slice before reading

As late as 1900 books were often sold with the folded edges of pages uncut. The reader sliced the folds open with a knife to turn the pages. Soft-cover books first appeared in Germany in 1841, but did not catch on in Britain and the USA until almost a century later. The first paperbacks were published by Penguin in the UK in 1935, offering cheap reading to a wider public. Another innovation was the book token, first issued in 1932, which became a popular Christmas present.

| 2500BC | AD 350 | 1045 | 1200s | 1450s | 1930s |
|---|---|---|---|---|---|
| EGYPTIAN SCROLL-BOOKS | OLDEST KNOWN CODEX, THE *CODEX SINAITICUS*, A BIBLE WRITTEN IN GREEK; 390 OF OVER 700 PAGES SURVIVE | CHINESE PRINTER BI SHENG INVENTS CLAY TYPE FOR PRINTING | PAPER FIRST USED FOR BOOKS, WHICH ARE STILL HANDWRITTEN | FIRST BOOKS PRINTED ON PRESSES, USING MOVABLE **TYPE** | PAPERBACKS BECOME POPULAR, AND DOMINATE THE BOOK TRADE BY THE 1950s |

# Printing press, 1454

Copying out books by hand took so long that books were very scarce. Very few people had books in their homes before 1500. Not many people went to school. Few poor people ever had the chance to learn to read, and many nobles never bothered. Knowledge stayed shut up in a few monasteries and libraries. So new ideas spread very slowly, usually in letters written by scholars.

## Gutenberg's idea

The inventor who made 'books for all' possible was a German called Johannes Gutenberg, who lived in the 1400s. He came up with a new method of printing. Printing from wood blocks (just as a child stamps pictures or words with a toy printing set) had been around since before 800 in China. Wood blocks were used in Europe to print playing cards, but it was a slow process.

The Chinese had invented movable **type** – individual characters made from clay that could be arranged on a metal plate. Chinese writing uses more than 5000 different characters, so printing was very slow. In German (and English), the alphabet has only 26 characters, or letters.

*An early hand printing press. The letters, or type, were arranged on a tray, called a forme. The press pushed a sheet of paper down onto the inked type.*

## How the press worked

Gutenberg's first bright idea was to take the screw press (an ancient invention used to crush olives and grapes) and turn it into a machine that would press a sheet of paper down on to an inked block. His second idea was to cast metal type (characters). Metal lasted longer than the clay type pioneered in China. It could also be reused.

As a boy, Gutenberg had watched workers making coins in the city mint, run by his father. He used this knowledge to make metal castings of letters, using a mixture of three metals – lead, tin and antimony. The letters could be arranged in any order to make words and set in lines on a holder, which was then brushed over with ink. A whole page could be inked at a time, and printed onto sheets of paper, over and over again. The letters could be lifted and rearranged as required.

## Right person, right time

Gutenberg was born into a Europe bursting with new ideas. It was the period historians call the **Renaissance**. People were eager for knowledge and wanted cheaper books. Paper was available and painters had developed oily inks, ideal for printing. Metalworking skills made casting type no problem. Plenty of people knew how to use screw press machines. Gutenberg's invention had a good chance of success.

The success was spectacular. Before 1450 there were probably no more than 1 million books in Europe. By 1500, about 9 million books had been printed. Today the number of books is too big to count.

### Johannes Gutenberg (139?–1468)

Gutenberg was born in Mainz, Germany in the 1390s and probably trained as a goldsmith in Strasbourg. He spent years developing his printing press, working in secret, but was always short of money. He had to take in partners and in 1448 he borrowed money from a lawyer named Fust. The partners quarrelled and just as Gutenberg was about to begin printing his first book, a 1282-page bible, Fust demanded his money back. Gutenberg had to hand over the business to Fust. His Bible was printed in 1455, but by then Gutenberg was ruined. He died in 1468, near-blind and quite poor.

| AD 700s | 1454–55 | 1476 | 1490 | 1604 | 1960s |
|---|---|---|---|---|---|
| CAPITAL (UPPERCASE) AND SMALL (LOWERCASE) LETTERS BEGAN TO BE USED | GUTENBERG PRINTS THE BIBLE USING HIS PRINTING PRESS | WILLIAM CAXTON STARTS THE FIRST PRINTING PRESS IN ENGLAND | FIRST ITALIC TYPE DESIGNED BY ALDUS MANUTIUS IN ITALY | FIRST ENGLISH DICTIONARY, BY A SCHOOLTEACHER NAMED ROBERT CAWDREY | COMPUTERIZED PHOTO-TYPESETTING BEGINS. MODERN MACHINES CAN SET 10,000 CHARACTERS A SECOND |

# Pencil, c. 1565

You can write with any tool that makes a mark. The Ancient Romans used sticks of lead to draw lines on papyrus sheets, to keep their handwriting straight when using pen and ink. Artists drew with sticks of charcoal (burnt wood), crayons (wax mixed with colouring) or chalks. They also used very thin brushes, and the word pencil comes from a Latin word meaning 'little brush'.

## Why pencils were needed

By the 1500s, more people were reading books (thanks to printing) and learning to write. They wanted to write letters or notes. Pens were messy. Quill pens had to be dipped into an ink bottle and, to avoid smudges, the writer sprinkled sand over the paper to dry the ink.

*This description of a pencil is written in Latin, the language of science in the 1500s. Graphite 'marking sticks' were put inside wooden holders.*

## Discovering graphite

What people wanted was a writing tool that did not need ink. Someone must have noticed that a soft form of **carbon**, called graphite, made marks on paper. Possibly it was a child. Conrad Gesner from Switzerland, wrote a description of a pencil in 1565, though this does not mean he invented it. His pencil was a wooden holder containing a rod of graphite mixed with clay. Because people thought graphite was lead, the rod of a pencil came to be called a 'lead'.

16

## Making pencils

The first pure graphite mine was in Cumberland, in northern England. People began digging out graphite there in 1564. The first pencils were made by hand, but by the 1800s machines were making them by the million. Machines mixed the graphite and clay, and squeezed out the 'leads' as long threads, like toothpaste. The leads were then sandwiched in wood and cut into pencil-lengths. Adding more clay made a harder pencil. More graphite in the mixture made a softer pencil.

*Making pencils in a factory. From the 19th century, demand for pencils was huge, and making pencils became a mechanized business.*

## And we still use pencils

Pencils were cheap and were soon in almost every home. By the late 1800s people could buy coloured pencils, pencil sharpeners, pencils with eraser tips, and mechanical 'propelling' pencils.

More than 10 billion pencils are made every year. Everyone uses pencils, from toddlers to pensioners. Even astronauts in space find them handy, because zero gravity does not affect pencil-writing. Divers can use pencils under water.

| PREHISTORIC TIMES | AD 1564 | 1565 | 1795 | 1850s | 1895 |
|---|---|---|---|---|---|
| CHARCOAL (BURNT STICKS) USED FOR DRAWING | PURE GRAPHITE MINE DISCOVERED IN NORTH WEST ENGLAND | FIRST WRITTEN DESCRIPTION OF A PENCIL, BY CONRAD GESNER | NICHOLAS JACQUES CONTE OF FRANCE MAKES AN IMPROVED PENCIL, USING POWDERED GRAPHITE AND CLAY | WILLIAM MONROE OF THE USA INVENTS A PENCIL-MAKING MACHINE | FIRST MECHANICAL OR 'PROPELLING' PENCIL, WITH A STOCK OF LEADS INSIDE A METAL BARREL |

# Semaphore, 1794

For thousands of years, the fastest way to send a message overland was by horse, or by pigeon (the Mongol leader Genghis Khan sent pigeon post in the early 1200s). Relays of messengers on horseback galloped with important letters. There was nothing faster until the 1790s.

## Watching for signals

People can see further than they can hear. Visual signals, such as fires, can be seen from a long way off. A chain of beacon fires, lit one after the other, could pass on an agreed signal. In 1588 beacons were used across southern England to warn of the approach of the Spanish Armada.

At sea, sailors hoisted flags to send messages in **code**. In the flag code, each coloured flag stood for a letter or number. Flag signalling worked only if ships were within sight of one another. It was aided by the invention of the telescope in the late 1500s.

*Semaphores like this one (smaller picture) were set up on top of towers, between 5 and 10 kilometres apart.*

## Getting the message

In wartime, communications are vital. In 1794 Claude Chappe, a French inventor, was asked to find a better way to send government orders at high speed. France had come though a violent revolution (1789) and was at war with most of Europe. It urgently needed new **technology**.

Chappe and his men set up windmill-like towers on hilltops, up to 20 km (12 miles) apart but within telescope range. Each tower bore a long bar, pivoted in the centre, with two smaller bars (also pivoted) at either end.

To send a message, the 'arms' could be moved to 49 different positions to represent letters and numbers. The observer in the next tower noted down the message, letter by letter, and then waggled the arms of his 'semaphore' to pass on the signal to the next tower in the chain.

## Success and weaknesses

The semaphore could send a message over 800 km (500 miles) in under 3 minutes. Its main weakness was that it worked only in daylight, and in good weather. It also needed a lot of people to run it.

### Claude Chappe (1763–1805)

Claude Chappe was born in France in 1763. His brother was a politician and backed Claude's idea for the semaphore (the word comes from Greek, and means 'bearing a sign'). The first test took place between Paris and Lille, and the semaphore brought within an hour news of a French army victory against the Austrians. Chappe was appointed government telegraph engineer, but rival inventors disputed his claim to the semaphore. He became depressed and killed himself in 1805.

The French government set up more than 550 semaphore towers across France. Britain hurriedly set up a similar system on church towers and hills. However, the war in Europe crippled any chance of commercial success, disappointing its inventor. The semaphore was used until the 1840s, when the electric telegraph (see pages 24–5) replaced it.

## Other uses for semaphore signals

The new railways (begun in the 1820s) took up the semaphore idea and 'moving arm' railway signals were used throughout the 20th century. Flag semaphore (a sailor holding two flags) was used at sea until the invention of radio in the early 1900s. A modern version of semaphore signalling is the bat-waving of groundcrews to direct aeroplanes moving on the ground.

| 1200 | 1588 | 1794 | 1840s | 1878 |
|---|---|---|---|---|
| GENGHIS KHAN USES HOMING PIGEONS TO CARRY MESSAGES | BEACON FIRES WARN ENGLAND OF THE SPANISH ARMADA'S APPROACH | CHAPPE SETS UP HIS FIRST SEMAPHORE STATIONS IN FRANCE | THE NEW ELECTRIC TELEGRAPH REPLACES SEMAPHORE<br><br>RAILWAYS ADOPT SEMAPHORE-TYPE SIGNALS | HELIOGRAPH (FLASHING LIGHT SIGNALS) USED BY ARMIES |

# Machine-powered printing, 1811

Printing is a mixture of old and new inventions. Leonardo da Vinci suggested a water-driven printing press in the early 1500s, not long after the first printing press had been invented. It worked, but wooden presses remained the usual method for the next 300 years.

## Machines take over

It was not until the early part of the Industrial Revolution (about 1750–1850) that steam power speeded up printing. The iron press was invented in about 1795 in Britain. Steam-driven presses were invented in 1811 by two Germans, Friedrich Koenig and Andreas Bauer. Their cylinder machines could print 1100 sheets an hour.

The new printing machines were four times as fast as the machines they replaced, and needed constant supplies of paper. In 1799 Louis Robert of France had invented a machine that turned a stream of wood pulp into a 15-metre-long roll of paper. But most printers still used sheets of paper.

In 1844 Richard Hoe invented a rotary press in which the **printing plate** with the **type** was fixed around a roller. This printed 8000 sheets an hour, eight times faster than the existing presses. In 1865, William Bullock invented a printing press fed by giant rolls of paper instead of sheets. Most modern printing machines print on a continuous web of paper, fed from a roll at very high speed. They print both sides of the paper at the same time.

## Setting the type

Typesetting (arranging letters to make words) was normally done by hand, using metal letters. In the 1820s typesetting machines with keyboards were used to select each piece of type, and were four times faster than hand-setting. In 1884 a German, Ottmar Mergenthaler, invented the Linotype machine. It had a keyboard on which a complete line of type could be arranged as a piece (or 'slug') of metal from movable moulds or matrices of the letters. The matrices could be used again while the 'line of type', properly spaced, was being printed. The Monotype machine of 1887, invented by Tolbert Lanston, cast and set individual pieces of type. Both machines greatly speeded up typesetting.

## Pictures, photography and computers

The invention of lithography ('stone-writing') made it easier to print pictures. Basically lithography is printing on a flat surface, using the principle that grease and water do not mix. It was invented in 1798 by Aloys Senefelder. He made a drawing in crayon on a stone. When the stone was wetted, the greasy drawing stayed dry and when inked, the drawing printed on to paper. Today metal plates have replaced the stone, and the image is a photographic one on film. The inked image is not printed directly onto paper, but is first 'offset' onto a rubber-covered cylinder, and from there onto paper or any other material.

*Modern printing machines produce everything from newspapers and books to textiles and sweet wrappers.*

Filmsetting using photographic film instead of metal type was a 1950s invention, but was based on 19th-century discoveries. Filmsetting revolutionized printing because it was so fast.

Computerization of printing began in the 1950s. Electronic phototypesetters are incredibly fast, producing over 35 million characters an hour. Text and pictures can be set up into pages using a computer program, and then turned into film. From this film guide, another machine then makes the metal plates from which books, magazines, newspapers and packaging are printed.

| **1798** | **1811** | **1844** | **1865** | **1904** | **1980s** |
|---|---|---|---|---|---|
| ALOYS SENEFELDER, A CZECH WRITER AND ARTIST, INVENTS LITHOGRAPHY | KOENIG AND BAUER'S FIRST STEAM PRESS | RICHARD HOE OF THE USA INVENTS THE ROTARY PRESS | CONTINUOUS REEL PRINTING USED FOR NEWSPAPERS | OFFSET PRINTING IS INVENTED IN THE USA | COMPUTERIZED **DIGITAL** TYPESETTING AND PAGE MAKE-UP REVOLUTIONIZE PRINTING |

# Braille, 1827

How can a blind person read? Before 1800, the only way was to have a sighted person read out loud. People who were born blind found it difficult to read, study and find work.

## Reading-by-touch

Louis Braille was born in 1809 in France. He was blinded at the age of three, following an accident in his father's shoe-making workshop. When he was ten, Louis was sent to the school for the blind in Paris. There children learned to read from handmade books with raised paper letters, tracing the letter shapes with their fingers. This was difficult and few children mastered it.

## A code for reading in the dark

When he was 12, Louis met an army officer named Captain Charles Barbier, who visited the school. Barbier had an idea which he thought might interest the teachers. He had invented an alphabet **code** using raised dots. The idea was that soldiers at night could read messages in darkness, by touch. They would not need lights and so would not give away their position to the enemy.

Unfortunately, soldiers found the code hard to learn and made too many mistakes. The army said no to Barbier's idea. But as he felt the pages of the code-book with his fingers, Louis Braille became excited. Why not have a dot alphabet for blind people?

*Braille writing is read by touch, running the fingers over the dots. A computer can translate ordinary print into Braille.*

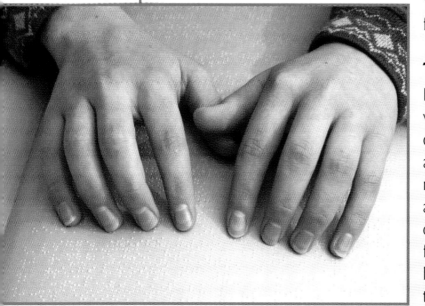

## The Braille system

It took Louis Braille six years to work out a system of six raised dots with sixty-three different arrangements for letters, numbers, punctuation marks and musical notes. He tried it out on his fellow students and found that most children learned it easily, though adults took a little longer.

In 1827, Braille published his first book with raised-dot words. It took time for his invention to catch on, but his system soon became known around the world simply as 'Braille'. Braille is still used not only for reading, but also for writing (using embossing pens or a six-key machine like a typewriter). A Braille printer can also be linked to a computer.

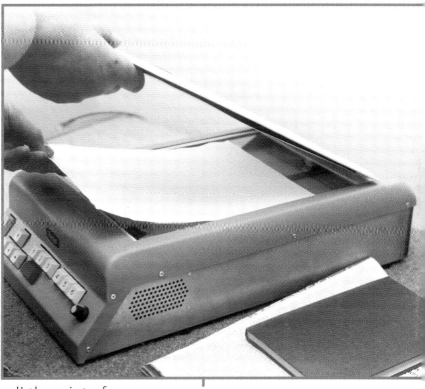

## New aids for visually impaired people

From the 1950s, progress in electronics has provided new aids for blind people or those with visual impairments. Many find handy-sized tape-players ('talking books') helpful or use optical **scanners**. These 'read' the print of a normal typeset book and turn the text into enlarged, raised letters that can be read by touch. More advanced aids 'read' print in a computerized, human-like voice.

*A Personal Reader uses a computerized voice to 'read' letters, magazines, books and bills. It can also store all of this information on disc.*

| 1784 | 1821 | 1827 | 1955 | 1960s | 1970s |
|---|---|---|---|---|---|
| PARIS SCHOOL FOR THE BLIND OPENED, THE FIRST IN THE WORLD | CHARLES BARBIER SHOWS LOUIS BRAILLE HIS RAISED DOT CODE | FIRST BRAILLE BOOK | FIRST TALKING BOOKS ON TAPE | COMPUTERIZED PRODUCTION OF BRAILLE BOOKS | OPTICAL SCANNERS TURN PRINT INTO RAISED LETTERS AND SOUNDS |

# Electric telegraph, 1837

Inventors playing about with home-made 'electrical machines' in the early 1800s discovered an interesting effect. An **electric current** passing through a wire could be shut on and off, and when this happened, apparatus attached to the wire might produce movement or noise. In 1816, a British inventor, Francis Ronalds, showed that electric current passing through wires strung from trees in his garden could make fibre balls twitch. He failed to persuade the government that here was the germ of a revolutionary communications system – peace had arrived after Napoleon's defeat at Waterloo.

## Putting signals through wires

In 1820 the Danish scientist Hans Oersted discovered **electromagnetism** – the fact that an electric current flowing through a wire would produce a **magnetic field**. In the 1830s, Michael Faraday and Joseph Henry discovered the useful reverse effect of electromagnetism. Moving a magnet near a coil of wire produced an electric current in the wire. Here was the breakthrough for a 'message by wire' system. Inventors in Britain, Germany, France, Russia and the USA raced to be first in making a telegraph or 'far-writing' machine.

*The inventor of the electric telegraph, Samuel Morse, also devised a code for sending messages along wires. Morse code became an international 'language'.*

## The first telegraph

In 1830 Joseph Henry, working in the USA, found that several small batteries together boosted a signal better than one big battery. Two British inventors, Charles Wheatstone and William Cooke, then managed to send a signal along a wire that was several miles long.

The inventor who won the race was Samuel Morse of the USA. Morse was an artist not a scientist, but he had great determination and chose expert partners in Leonard Gale, a chemist, and Alfred Vail, an engineer. By 1837 they had a working telegraph. The telegraph worked by opening and closing an electrical circuit rapidly, to produce signals that sped along a wire. At the other end the signals were turned into clicking sounds or made marks on paper.

Morse's secret was a **code** of dots and dashes – ever after known as Morse code. In 1844 he tapped out the words 'What hath God wrought', and the message flashed instantly from Washington DC to Baltimore – a distance of 65 km (45 miles). It was magical.

*Cables being packed ready for the second attempt at laying a permanent cable across the Atlantic.*

## Impact of the telegraph

The telegraph had enormous impact. In the USA, its incredible speed put the **Pony Express** out of business practically overnight. Soon it spanned continents, linking the world by wire. The 'cable' became the best way to send urgent messages.

Morse code was adopted world-wide in 1851. Its most famous signal (SOS – three dots, three dashes, three dots) remained the emergency 'Mayday' code for ships at sea until replaced by **satellite** communication in 1999.

### Samuel Morse (1791–1872)

Samuel Finley Breese Morse was born in Massachusetts, USA, in 1791. A graduate of Yale University, he studied art and became a successful portrait painter. He spent ten years tinkering with the electric telegraph, making his own equipment from scraps of wire and cotton thread. When stumped by science, he took partners who knew more than he did. He badgered Congress until it agreed to test his new invention. It was a huge success, though Morse later sold his **patent** rights.

| 1837 | 1844 | 1851 | 1866 | 1872 | 1874 |
|---|---|---|---|---|---|
| MORSE PATENTS HIS FIRST TELEGRAPH | FIRST DEMONSTRATION OF MORSE-VAIL TELEGRAPH | FIRST CROSS-CHANNEL TELEGRAPH CABLE | FIRST TRANSATLANTIC TELEGRAPH CABLE | JOSEPH STEARNS INVENTS THE DUPLEX (TWO MESSAGES SIMULTANEOUSLY) | THOMAS EDISON'S QUADRUPLEX TELEGRAPH (FOUR MESSAGES AT THE SAME TIME) |

# Postal service, 1840

Letters carried by runners or horse-riders travelled surprisingly quickly. Riders changing horses at intervals could cover 160 km (100 miles) in a day. Private letter-carrying services began in Europe in about 1300. One of the biggest, in Vienna, Austria, employed 20,000 people as mail-carriers.

*In a modern mail-sorting office, machines handle the mail far more often than people. A human hand though still delivers each letter to the letterbox.*

## Letter post

In the 1600s governments began setting up national mail systems. In 1680 the city of London had a penny post, which the government took over when it proved profitable. The receiver of the letter paid the charge when the letter arrived.

In 1840 Rowland Hill, a retired British schoolteacher, had a better idea. The sender could buy a fixed-charge stamp before posting the letter. Also letters should be enclosed in envelopes – not just folded and sealed with a blob of wax. This was the start of the modern mail service.

## Handling the mail

Hill's stamps were a huge success, and soon most countries had them. Letters were sent in their millions, along with greetings cards – the first Christmas card appeared in 1843. The new railways and steamships carried mail swiftly.

The ever-growing mountain of mail was collected and sorted in post offices. For 100 years, sorting was done mostly by hand. Staff read the address on the envelopes and packages, and put them into bags. In 1963 the US Post Office introduced ZIP (zonal improvement plan) **codes** for mail, with numbers which a machine could read. Other countries brought in their own postcodes to speed up automated mail handling.

## The first stamps

Before 1840, mail was ink-stamped to show it was paid for. The first adhesive stamps were issued in Great Britain on May 6 1840. They were a one-penny black and a two-penny blue, each bearing the head of Queen Victoria. The USA issued its first stamps on July 1 1847. By 1860, almost every country had begun using stamps on mail. People started collecting stamps almost at once – the first stamp catalogue for collectors was published in 1861.

*The British one-penny black stamp of 1840, the world's first 'sticky stamp' for letters.*

## The mail sorter

In a modern sorting office, mail is sorted by size and arranged so all the envelopes face the same way. The stamps are cancelled and postmarked. Machines using an electronic system called optical character recognition (OCR) read the postcode. Another machine marks a **barcode** on the mail, so that a third machine can read the code and sort the letters automatically.

The latest US mail sorting machine (1999), marvellously named the Delivery Bar Code Sorter Input/Output Sub-System, does all three jobs. It can read addresses on mail of almost any size, print barcodes, weed out badly written addresses and send them off for deciphering, and sort mail by town and street (ready for the postperson to deliver). It can sort 40,000 pieces of mail an hour.

| 1609 | 1680 | 1840 | 1919 | 1963 | 1999 |
|------|------|------|------|------|------|
| ENGLISH GOVERNMENT TAKES CONTROL OF MAIL SERVICE | WILLIAM DOCKWRA STARTS PENNY POST IN LONDON | ROWLAND HILL INVENTS THE ONE-CHARGE STAMP POST | FIRST REGULAR INTERNATIONAL MAIL (LONDON–PARIS) | FIRST ZIP CODES IN THE USA | FIRST FULLY AUTOMATED MAIL SORTER |

# Fax machine, 1843

Fax is short for facsimile ('copy'). A fax machine is used to send documents and pictures along a telephone wire, as a series of coded electrical pulses. Using a fax machine, people can exchange documents around the world in minutes.

## Early experiments

The idea for a copy-sending machine dates from 1843. In this year a Scot named Alexander Bain **patented** a machine that used a swinging pendulum to trace an image or write a message on paper. The message was sent by electrical impulses and recreated by a second 'receiving' pendulum. Bain hoped to use the telegraph (see pages 24–5) as a means of sending pictures, but never actually sent a fax message.

## Attempts at telegraph-faxing

In 1851 another British inventor, Frederick Blakewell, demonstrated a fax machine similar to Bain's but with cylinders. It was one of the stars of the Great Exhibition of arts and sciences held that year in London. The French set up the world's first fax line for letters in 1865, using a remarkable machine invented by an Italian churchman named Giovanni Caselli. The Caselli fax was also tried in Britain, between London and Manchester.

This brilliant invention was then forgotten. It lost out to the telegraph. Governments and businesses were spending money on telegraph links for sending Morse code. They were not interested in the fax system, even though it was potentially more useful.

*Arthur Korn of Germany in 1906 with the fax machine he invented to send photographs by wire.*

## Pictures by wire

The invention of the telephone (see pages 32–33) brought a huge expansion in the wires linking towns and cities. Long-distance phone

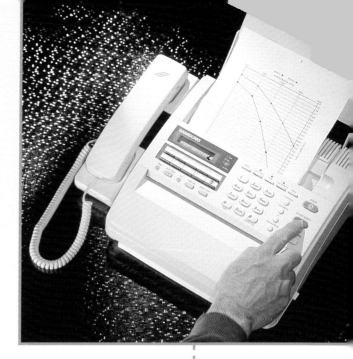

calls were being made by the early 1900s, and in 1902 a German scientist named Arthur Korn invented 'photoelectric' **scanning**, a fax system for sending photographs by wire. Korn's invention was taken up quickly by German newspapers. By the 1920s, newspapers across the USA were using a fax system developed by the American Telephone & Telegraph Company to send and receive news photos by wire.

*A modern fax-phone can send a picture or a letter in seconds to another machine anywhere in the world.*

Two problems with early faxes were fuzzy pictures and slow speed. All the data making up a photograph (consisting of black and white dots) had to be scanned, stored and transmitted using **analogue technology**. In the 1920s it took seven minutes to fax one photo.

## Speeding up

**Digital** machines, which store signals in numerical or **binary** code, were developed in the 1960s. By the 1980s they were proving invaluable to businesses for sending letters, pictures and technical details across thousands of kilometres more or less instantaneously.

Using computer technology, electronic digital faxes code the scanned image into binary digits (bits) and transmit them through a **modem**. The scanner moves over the page, measuring the brightness of the spots (called pixels) line by line. This data is compressed (made smaller), transmitted through a phone line and then 'unsqueezed' to print out a copy of the original image on paper. Modern machines can fax a page in less than 10 seconds.

| 1843 | 1902 | 1922 | 1930s | 1980s |
|---|---|---|---|---|
| ALEXANDER BAIN PATENTS THE FIRST FAX MACHINE | PHOTO-FAX SYSTEM INVENTED BY ARTHUR KORN OF GERMANY | FIRST IMAGES FAXED ACROSS THE ATLANTIC, BY RADIO | FACSIMILE TELEGRAPH (TELEPHOTO) MACHINES USED FOR NEWS PHOTOGRAPHS | FASTER DIGITAL FAX MACHINES REPLACE ANALOGUE MACHINES |

# Typewriter, 1868

The typewriter became useful when the pace of business life increased so much that people's handwriting could no longer keep up. And we still see the typewriter's legacy in front of us – on our computer keyboard.

*This early typewriter has the still-used key arrangement (look at the top line of black keys). The carriage moved the paper so each key hit a fresh space.*

## The writing machine

In 1714 an Englishman named Henry Mills invented a writing machine, but found to his dismay that no one wanted him to build it. Writing by hand was quite fast enough. Governments employed clerks to write letters and make copies in neat **longhand**. If really busy, clerks used **shorthand** for taking down quick notes, writing them up later. Until the 1870s every business had rooms full of clerks on stools, writing at desks. Most were men.

## The first typewriter

In the 1800s inventors wondered if blind people could use a machine to tap out words. Printers were experimenting with machines for setting **type**. The idea was to use keys (like those of a piano), moving wires up and down to print letters on paper moved sideways by a carriage device.

Christopher Latham Scholes, an American journalist, built a machine with the help of Carlos Glidden and Samuel W Soulé, and patented it in 1868. Unfortunately, the keys kept jamming.

## The QWERTY keyboard

Scholes got some fresh ideas after reading about another typewriter designed in Britain. By 1870 he had rearranged the letters on his machine's keyboard. The arrangement he chose was known as QWERTY. Commonly used letters in English were spaced apart, so it was difficult to jam the keys.

## Typewriters take over

The new machine was a hit. Scholes proved it could out-type rival machines. Soon typewriters were being installed in offices in the USA and Europe. They were easy to use. The ink was on a ribbon that could be quickly changed and the typewriter's ability to make lots of copies, using **carbon** paper, was also useful. Firms hired men and, increasingly, women to work as typists. This was one of the least expected effects of Scholes' invention – it created new jobs for women.

*'Golfball' typewriters, ideal for home use, were lighter to move around than most office machines.*

For a hundred years, the typewriter ruled supreme. In the 1920s, office typing was made easier and faster by James Smathers' electric typewriter, which had an electric motor to drive the 'touch-sensitive' keys. The electric typewriter never completely ousted the manual machine though. By the 1960s manufacturers were trying new and faster printing systems – such as the 'golfball', a sphere containing letters that moved while the typewriter carriage stayed still.

But the typewriter's day was coming to an end. In the 1980s, along came the PC (Personal Computer) and the word processor. Very quickly, the typewriter became an antique – though some people still use them. A manual typewriter goes on working even in a power cut!

| 1841 | 1868 | 1889 | 1920s | 1960s | 1980s |
|---|---|---|---|---|---|
| THE INKED RIBBON IS INVENTED BY ALEXANDER BAIN | SCHOLES TYPEWRITER IS **PATENTED** IN THE USA | FIRST PORTABLE TYPEWRITER, THE AMERICAN BLICK | FIRST ELECTRIC TYPEWRITERS | GOLFBALL TYPEWRITER, WITH THE TYPE ON A ROTATING BALL, AND FIRST ELECTRONIC TYPEWRITER, FROM IBM | WORD PROCESSORS REPLACE TYPEWRITERS |

# Telephone, 1876

By 1860 the telephone seemed an obvious follow-on from the telegraph (see pages 24–5). If electrical pulses through a wire could make clicks, then surely they could reproduce the human voice? Telegraphs could send signals, music, even squeaks – but not speech.

## The sound problem

There were big problems to overcome. The many sounds of human speech had to be 'captured', coded electrically, and then decoded so someone at the other end of a wire could hear and understand them.

What was needed was a **microphone** and a receiver. Sound waves in the air would make a thin plate or **diaphragm** move or vibrate. This movement could be turned into electrical pulses and sent through a wire. Then, using a second diaphragm to 'echo' the vibrations, the pulses would be turned back into sounds. In the 1860s one inventor tried using sausage skins as diaphragms, but gave up!

## The first phone call

A teacher, Alexander Graham Bell, cracked the problem in 1875. Bell was a talented teacher of the deaf in Boston, Massachusetts. He was trying to use the harmonic telegraph (a telegraph with vibrating reeds) to help deaf people hear.

As so often in the story of inventions, an accident opened the door to success. Bell and his technical assistant Thomas Watson were working in adjoining rooms, linked by wires. Watson pulled a reed free from his machine and, as it broke, Bell heard the 'snap' through his receiver. This accident spurred them on to build their first telephone.

*Alexander Graham Bell speaking into the mouthpiece of his first telephone (1876). It could both send and receive voice signals.*

The great day came in March 1876. Bell was in his laboratory, nervously waiting to test the telephone. In his anxiety, he upset some acid and called out 'Mr Watson, come here. I want you!' Watson came running from the next room. He had heard every word clearly over the wire.

## The phone catches on

Bell only narrowly pipped a rival inventor, Elisha Gray, to the post in **patenting** the telephone. It was Bell who became famous as 'the telephone man'. He demonstrated his phone on both sides of the Atlantic Ocean. By 1880 there were more than 30,000 phones in use. Dial phones appeared in 1896, so people could now call a local number direct.

Americans were the most enthusiastic phone users. Long-distance lines crossed the continent – people's voices were loud and clear, thanks to new booster relays. By 1910 there were 7 million phones in the USA, and call boxes were installed in stores and in street booths.

The telephone transformed the use of communications. You can now call a friend direct in almost any place in the world, your voice travelling through **fibre-optic cables** and 'bouncing' off **satellites**.

### Alexander Graham Bell (1847–1922)

Bell was born in Scotland but moved to the USA, to teach deaf people. After he successfully demonstrated his telephone in 1876, he set up the Bell Telephone Company. In 1878 an improved microphone invented by Thomas Alva Edison made the Bell phone even better. Bell later improved Edison's phonograph, the first sound recording machine. He died in 1922.

*Telephones like this began to appear in people's homes in the 1930s. The caller 'dialled' a number using the finger-holes.*

| 1876 | 1890 | 1900 | 1956 | 1965 | 1988 |
|---|---|---|---|---|---|
| BELL INVENTS THE TELEPHONE | ALMON STROWGER INVENTS THE AUTOMATIC EXCHANGE | FIRST LONG-DISTANCE CALLS | FIRST TRANSATLANTIC TELEPHONE CABLE | FIRST SATELLITE PHONE CALLS | FIRST UNDERSEA FIBRE-OPTIC CABLES |

# Fountain pen, 1884

The fountain pen, or cartridge pen, was invented in the 1880s when someone got tired of having inky fingers!

Ink was first used in China and Egypt about 2500BC. People made ink by mixing soot from oil lamps with sticky plant gums. The Egyptians used reed pens. The Greeks and Romans liked metal styluses for writing in clay or wax, and ink pens with split-end nibs. In the Middle Ages in Europe, goose feathers were used to make quill pens – people carried penknives to sharpen the nibs. Quill pens were used until the 1800s.

## Inky fingers

A quill pen had to be dipped into an ink pot. So did the cheap wooden pens used by 19th-century schoolchildren. Inky fingers were common! What if a pen had its own ink pot? Various inventors tried to make an ink-filled 'fountain' pen. Either the ink was too thin and the pen spurted out a 'fountain' of ink, or it was too thick, and the pen refused to write at all.

## Mr Waterman's pen

The first really good fountain pen was made in 1884 by an American named Lewis E Waterman. He sold insurance, and had tried various 'improved' ink-filled pens, but they leaked, spoiling his forms and his shirt cuffs. So he designed his own pen, filling it with ink from an eye-dropper bottle.

Later fountain pens had a rubber sac inside for the ink, and were filled by a lever to siphon ink from the bottle into the sac. The fountain pen looked smart, so people wanted to own one. It was convenient – you could carry it around and write letters, sign cheques or fill in forms wherever you were.

*This close-up of a fountain pen writing shows how ink flows down the split in the nib.*

## Cartridges, balls and other tips

Most modern pens have ink-filled, drop-in cartridges. Other pens, such as the ballpoint, the felt tip and the fibre tip, also have their own ink supply, but differ in the design of their writing points.

The modern ballpoint pen appeared in 1938. Invented by Hungarian brothers, Laszlo and Georg Biró, the ballpoint used thick printing ink which dried almost as soon as it hit the paper (so no smudges). Many people, though not some teachers, liked the smooth ball action. Felt-tipped pens were a 1960s invention.

*The felt tip pen, which appeared in the 1960s, is a modern version of the ancient reed pen.*

| 1884 | 1904 | 1927 | 1938 | 1953 | 1963 |
|------|------|------|------|------|------|
| LEWIS WATERMAN DESIGNS HIS FOUNTAIN PEN | GEORGE PARKER (USA) INVENTS THE LEVER-FILL FOR PENS | THE INK CARTRIDGE IS INVENTED | BIRÓ BROTHERS MAKE THEIR FIRST BALLPOINT PEN | MASS-PRODUCED BALLPOINTS GO ON SALE IN FRANCE | JAPANESE INVENT THE FELT-TIPPED PEN |

# Photocopier, 1938

If a person living in 1800 wanted to send the same letter to ten people, the only way was to copy it ten times. Copying was slow and boring work. It kept thousands of workers occupied.

## Carbon copies

Early in the 19th century, a faster method was invented – ink-soaked **carbon** paper. A clerk slipped a sheet of carbon paper between two sheets of writing paper, wrote on the top sheet – and hey presto, there was a 'carbon-copy' on the bottom sheet. Carbon paper became really useful when offices began using typewriters in the 1870s. A typist could make several copies at once, using several sheets of carbon paper placed between plain sheets.

## Duplication

In 1888 a machine called the duplicator was invented to make multiple copies from an original document. It was made in London by a Hungarian named David Gestetner, who used a typewriter to punch a waxed-fibre sheet in order to produce a stencil. The stencil was inked and a paper-covered roller pushed over it to print each copy. The Roneo machine of 1900, invented by a Czech named A D Klaber, was faster because it used a roller-drum, turned by a handle. It could roll off 5000 copies from one original.

A new and useful accessory to deal with the mounting piles of paper copies was the paper clip, invented in about 1900!

## How the photocopier was invented

Carbon paper was fine for copying new letters. But how could you copy an old one? Photographing it was messy and too expensive for office or school. During the 1930s a young American physicist named Chester Carlson spent his spare time trying to invent a clean, fast 'photocopying' machine to copy patent drawings. He worked in a **patent** office. Rather than use chemicals or photographs, he experimented with xerography ('dry copying'). This uses electrical charges, light and heat to transfer images from one sheet of paper to another.

## How a photocopier works

It works like this. A light system (a lamp, lens and mirrors) projects an image of the document onto a metal drum, which carries a negative (−) electrical charge. The light removes the charge from all but the dark areas of the image, which keep their negative charge. Particles of ink (toner) with a positive (+) charge are put on the drum and stick to the dark areas of the image, because (−) and (+) charges attract each other. The copy of the image is transferred onto paper and fixed by heat before it comes out of the machine.

## Slow success

Carlson succeeded in 1938. He reproduced on paper a copy of a handwritten date and a place name ('10–22–38 Astoria'). His basic equipment included a glass slide, a light bulb, a light-sensitive metal plate and some moss spores (his toner), which stuck to the image. The Second World War began in 1939 and Carlson did not get very far with his photocopier until 1947, when the Haloid Company, later the Xerox Corporation, took up the idea.

*Chester Carlson (1906-68) was turned down many times before he found a company to sell his new photocopier.*

The first office copiers were expensive, and needed special paper. Copiers did not become common until the 1960s when plain paper copiers went on sale. Carlson, however, did well from selling his invention, and unlike many other inventors became a millionaire.

| 1888 | 1938 | 1947 | 1958 | 1960s | 1970s |
|---|---|---|---|---|---|
| FIRST STENCIL-DUPLICATING MACHINE INVENTED BY DAVID GESTETNER | CARLSON'S FIRST SUCCESSFUL TEST COPY | HALOID (LATER XEROX) BUYS THE RIGHTS TO XEROGRAPHY | FIRST XEROX OFFICE COPIERS GO ON SALE | FIRST PLAIN PAPER COPIERS | COLOUR COPIERS COME INTO USE |

# Communications satellite, 1960

In 1945 writer Arthur C Clarke made what seemed like a crazy prediction. He said that in a few years **satellites** orbiting the Earth would provide world coverage for telephone calls and television. No satellite had yet been fired into space. Even in 1956 leading astronomers were still saying space travel just would not happen.

## Satellites go into space

In 1957 the Russians launched *Sputnik I*, the first earth satellite. Soon Clarke was proved right. He had written about satellites in **geostationary orbit** – positioned above the equator at a height of 35,785 km (22,365 miles), orbiting 'in time' with the Earth and so maintaining the same position over the surface. Such a satellite is a fixed target for signals from the ground, relaying them back across oceans and continents.

*Telstar (1962) relayed TV pictures across the Atlantic Ocean. The 63-kg satellite was followed by Telstar 2 in 1963.*

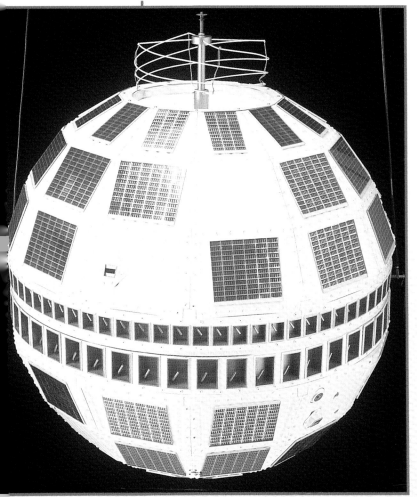

## First comsats

The USA launched the first communications satellite or 'comsat' in 1960. It was called *Echo I* and was a shiny balloon 30 metres (33 yards) round. Crude though it was, *Echo* proved that it was possible to bounce **radio** and television signals off a satellite in space and back to the ground.

In July 1962 the Americans launched a much better comsat called *Telstar*. For the first time television viewers in the USA could watch live pictures from Europe. *Telstar* became famous – it even had a pop hit written in its honour. It could handle just one TV transmission and 60 phone calls.

## Entertainment and education

Communications satellites were successful because people wanted to see live events such as the Olympic Games. India and other developing countries used satellite TV to educate people who lived in remote regions without proper schools and colleges.

Satellites are expensive to build and launch, but television companies are willing to pay a lot of money for satellite time. Some companies started their own satellite broadcasting channels, beaming programmes around the world into the homes of people with small dish **antennae**.

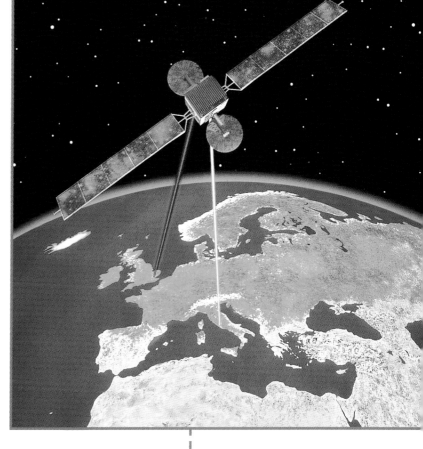

*Today a ring of satellites orbit the Earth, each one relaying TV channels and phone calls from transmitters to receivers.*

## Satellite power

Satellite TV broadcasters now rival ground-based terrestrial stations. Satellite power grew and grew. By the 1980s the Earth was ringed by Intelsat communications satellites, each able to relay 33,000 telephone calls and as many as 60 television channels. The power of satellites has gone on growing.

| 1957 | 1960 | 1962 | 1965 | 1980s | 1990s |
|------|------|------|------|-------|-------|
| FIRST EARTH SATELLITE | *ECHO I* PROVES SATELLITES WORK | *TELSTAR* BEAMS LIVE PICTURES ACROSS THE ATLANTIC OCEAN | EARLY BIRD, THE WORLD'S FIRST COMMERCIAL COMMUNICATIONS SATELLITE | INTELSAT SATELLITES BOOST COMMUNICATIONS CAPACITY | SATELLITE BROADCASTING WORLD-WIDE |

# Mobile phone, 1979

Until the 1920s, all telephones relied on wires to carry voice signals as electrical impulses. There was a 'wireless' way to transmit sounds – **radio**. From it developed something seen everywhere today, the mobile phone.

## Radio phones

The first phones without wires were radio phones, which sent signals through the air as radio waves. Reginald Fessenden spoke the first words 'on the air' in 1900 in the USA, though his signal travelled less than 1.6 km (1 mile). By 1906 he was playing the violin over the airwaves! As short-wave radio **technology** improved, portable radio phones were tried out by the Detroit police in 1921. Car phones became popular with highway patrols in a number of countries.

In 1946 a mobile phone service was tried in St Louis, in the USA. In 1947 Bell Laboratories came up with the idea of using transmitter 'cells' to pass on phone messages from one mobile phone to the next. The cell-phone sends and receives radio signals to and from transmitters arranged in areas called cells. The **antenna**-transmitter in the nearest cell picks up the call and passes it on to the next cell, and into the main telephone network. Without modern electronics, the early experiments were not very effective – only one person could speak at a time.

## The changing phone

By the 1960s, many people had more than one phone at home. But almost all phones were plugged in. There were cordless phones, but the caller could not wander far from the base unit, which was wired into the phone line. People wanted phones that they could take anywhere. These were made possible by rapid changes in **telecommunications**.

The first automatic telephone exchange was opened in Nebraska, USA, in 1921. It was mechanical and relied on **analogue** technology. The world's first electronic phone exchange began working in New Jersey, USA, in 1965. Computerized **digital** technology, in which information was represented by electrical pulses, made the phone

system faster and more efficient, and turned the cell-phone into a truly mobile personal communications device.

## The cell-phone reappears

The American city of Chicago tried out Bell's electronic cell-phone system in 1978. In 1979 the Ericsson Company of Sweden demonstrated their new cell-phone, and within two years there was a mobile phone network across Scandinavia. Soon mobile phones could be seen on city streets everywhere as cell networks were set up.

It was easy to 'listen in' on the early phones, which used analogue signals. Modern digital phones are much more secure from eavesdroppers. Analogue signals are changed into digital **binary code**, giving clearer transmission. The code is then changed back into analogue signals so the sounds can be heard. Phones with **microchips** can also store numbers and access information.

*Mobile phones in a range of models, old and new, are used for everything from 'I missed the bus' calls to big business deals.*

## The global phone network

In the 1990s mobile phones became a common sight all over the world, and were especially popular with young people. In 1999 the first new 'media phones' came on the market, based on WAP (Wireless Applications Protocol). With a media phone, a person can not only talk to other phone users, but also access the **Internet**, and send and receive email (see pages 42–3).

| 1938 | 1949 | 1970 | 1979 | 1983 | 1999 |
|------|------|------|------|------|------|
| AL GROSS OF USA INVENTS 'WALKIE TALKIE' | AL GROSS INVENTS TELEPHONE PAGER OR 'BLEEPER' | DIRECT DIALLING BETWEEN NEW YORK CITY AND LONDON | ERICSSON MOBILE PHONE LAUNCHED IN SWEDEN | FIRST COMMERCIAL CELL-PHONE SYSTEM IN THE USA | WAP PHONES EXTEND RANGE OF PHONE SERVICES BY OFFERING INTERNET ACCESS |

# Email, 1982

There are all kinds of ways to send messages – by letter, by telegraph, by telephone, by fax. The newest, and the one that has grown most rapidly, is email.

## How email began

Email grew in the 1980s as a by-product of the **Internet**. The Internet grew from a network of computers, linked so that information could be exchanged between them.

At first the Internet was used only by computer experts in universities and colleges, but from 1991 commercial companies began to offer Internet access to anyone with a computer, a **modem** and a phone connection. The modem was a 1950s invention which found its place in **telecommunications** in the 1980s. It connects a computer to the phone lines, allowing it to exchange information with other computers.

## The growth of email

By the 1980s many millions of people all over the world had phones in their homes, and millions were also buying cheap PCs for home use. Schools, too, were going online to use this new source of information and exchange. Everything was in place for another communications revolution.

A popular use for the new computer network was to send messages as electronic mail, or email. Often teenagers were the first to have fun with this new **technology**. They began sending messages to each other. Businesses soon realized the importance of this new super-fast communications system.

## Using email

Anyone with an Internet connection can have their own email address, from their Internet Service Provider (ISP). The provider acts as a collector for all mail, re-routing it to the right address. To send an email, you open a mail program on your computer, and type a message with the correct email address of the person or persons it is going to. An email can include attachments (documents or pictures). Click on 'Send', and away the email goes.

An email is a sequence of signals. The data in the file you created is transmitted **digitally** through the phone system by a modem. This changes computer data into electrical signals that can travel along metal wires, **fibre-optic cables** or through the air as **radio** waves. The email is collected by the ISP. When the receiver wants to read their email, they access the ISP through the Internet, and open their mail program. Incoming mail appears in the Inbox, and can be read on screen, saved or printed out.

Some emails you may not want. There is junk email just as there is junk mail. But email is very useful to people who need to exchange information quickly. People working from home, for example, can send letters or even books at the click of a button on their computer mouse.

*People can access the Internet from any computer linked to the phone network. Emails have become part of business, school and home life for many computer users.*

| 1958 | 1982 | 1980s | 1989 | 1991 | 1990s |
|---|---|---|---|---|---|
| INVENTION OF THE MODEM | WESTERN UNION STARTS EASYLINK EMAIL SERVICE IN THE USA | MORE PEOPLE BUY PCS FOR HOME AND SCHOOL USE | CREATION OF THE WORLD WIDE WEB (WWW) ON THE INTERNET | FIRMS START OFFERING INTERNET CONNECTION | GROWTH OF EMAIL IN MANY COUNTRIES |

# Timeline

| | |
|---|---|
| **Prehistoric times** | Charcoal (burnt sticks) used for drawing |
| **3500–3000BC** | Cuneiform writing invented in Sumeria |
| **2500BC** | First Egyptian scroll-books |
| **2300BC** | Oldest known map |
| **600BC** | Latin alphabet introduced |
| **AD 105** | First paper made in China |
| **868** | First printed book, the Chinese *Diamond Sutra* |
| **1200** | First paper books, still handwritten |
| **1454–5** | First book (the Bible) printed by Johannes Gutenberg on a press, using movable **type** |
| **1565** | First written description of a pencil |
| **1570** | First book of maps, or atlas |
| **1680** | William Dockwra starts penny post in London |
| **1794** | Claude Chappe invents Semaphore |
| **1811** | Koenig and Bauer's first steam printing press |
| **1827** | First Braille book produced by Louis Braille |
| **1837** | Samuel Morse **patents** his first telegraph |
| **1840** | Englishman Rowland Hill invents the one-charge stamp post |
| **1843** | Alexander Bain patents first fax machine |
| **1844** | First demonstration of Morse-Vail telegraph |

| | |
|---|---|
| **1844** | Richard Hoe of the USA invents the rotary printing press |
| **1868** | American Christopher Latham Scholes patents first typewriter |
| **1876** | Alexander Graham Bell invents the telephone |
| **1884** | Lewis Waterman designs first fountain pen |
| **1902** | Arthur Korn of Germany invents photo-fax system |
| **1920s** | First electric typewriters |
| **1938** | Biró brothers make first ballpoint pen |
| | Chester Carlson produces first successful photocopy |
| **1940s** | Recycling, or reuse, of waste paper begins |
| **1947** | Radio phones used by US highway police |
| **1957** | *Sputnik 1*, first earth **satellite**, launched |
| **1958** | **Modem** invented |
| **1960s** | Computerized photo-typesetting begins |
| **1960** | *Echo 1*, first communications satellite, launched |
| **1965** | First satellite phone calls |
| **1970s** | Colour photocopiers first come into use |
| **1979** | Ericsson mobile phone launched in Sweden |
| **1980s** | Computerized **digital** typesetting and page make-up revolutionize printing |
| **1982** | Western Union starts its Easylink email service in the USA |

# Glossary

**analogue** representation of numerical or physical quantities by physical variables, such as electrical voltage changes

**antenna** device for collecting electrical and radio signals in the atmosphere, also called an aerial

**barcode** striped marking with coded information that can be read electronically when a laser scans the barcode

**binary** digit 0 or 1 in the binary system, which works from base of two, using only the digits 0 and 1

**Buddhist** followers of the teachings of the Buddha, Siddattha Gotama, who lived in India from about 563 to 483BC

**carbon** natural substance (charcoal, soot, diamonds and coal are all forms of carbon)

**code** system of symbols or signs used for storing and sending information; a code may be secret or one made for a machine to understand

**diaphragm** dividing layer, made of flexible material, which in a microphone vibrates to transmit (send) or receive sound waves

**digital** in computers, recording information in signals called 'bits'. A digital watch shows numbers on a screen, not by hands moving around a dial.

**electric current** the flow of electricity through a metal wire

**electrode** metal plate through which electric current enters or leaves a battery or vacuum tube; either an anode or a cathode

**electromagnetism** force produced when an electric current flows through a coil of wire

**fibre-optic cable** means of sending light-signals very fast along thin glass or plastic tubes bundled together; used for communications

**geometry** branch of mathematics to do with measuring and comparing lines, angles and figures

**geostationary orbit** placing a satellite in space at such a height and speed that it stays in position above the same point on the Earth's surface

**hieroglyphics** picture-writing, used in Ancient Egypt and the Americas; a hieroglyph stood for a word, a sound or an idea

**latitude** the distance of a place (in degrees) north or south of the equator

**longhand** writing by hand, with a pen or pencil

**longitude** the distance of a place (in degrees) east or west of a line linking the North and South Poles (now measured from the Greenwich meridian, 0°)

**magnetic field** lines of force around the poles of a magnet, seen when iron filings are scattered around a magnet

**microchip** tiny electronic device, with circuits built up on a wafer of silicon

**modem** device which links a computer to the telephone system, allowing computers to communicate with one another through the Internet

**patent** description of a new invention which the inventor presents to a 'patent office'; no other person can copy the patent without permission

**Phoenician** person from ancient land of Phoenicia, in what is now Lebanon

**Pony Express** mail service set up in the United States in 1860, using riders on fast horses

**printing plate** metal plate carrying a photographically imposed image of letters and pictures, the part of a printing press that transfers the ink onto the paper either directly or indirectly

**radio** sending sounds through the air electronically, without wires

**Renaissance** period in European history (roughly 1350 to 1550) noted for new ideas in art and science, and rediscovery of ancient learning

**satellite** small planet or spacecraft in orbit around a larger body e.g. Earth around the Sun

**scan** to look at every part of something; an electronic scanner sweeps a beam across a surface to pick up any data it can read

**scroll** book written on a long piece of paper rolled on two sticks, and unrolled to read

**shorthand** system of fast writing, using shortened forms of words and symbols

**sign** anything that gives information; a sign can be a mark or picture

**technology** putting science to practical use, using methods and machines made by inventors to make people's lives better

**telecommunications** all the means of sending messages over long distances electronically, such as by telephone, radio and the Internet

**type** letters, numbers and other characters (symbols) used in printing

# Index

# Titles in the *GREAT INVENTIONS* series include:

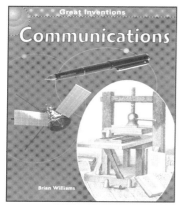

Hardback      0 431 13240 2

Hardback      0 431 13241 0

Hardback      0 431 13233 X

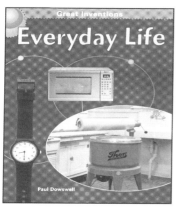

Hardback      0 431 13232 1

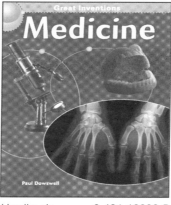

Hardback      0 431 13230 5

Hardback      0 431 13242 9

Hardback      0 431 13243 7

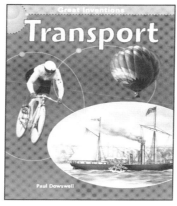

Hardback      0 431 13231 3

Find out about the other titles in this series on our website www.heinemann.co.uk/library